Using Electricity

Electricity makes my car go.

Electricity makes my train go.

Electricity makes my boat go.

Electricity makes my torch go.

Electricity makes my fan go.

Electricity makes my keyboard go.

Electricity makes my clock go.

Electricity makes my hair go.